Good Food

New Zealand Style

Chanel

Restaurant Directory

Albany Inn
276 Main Road, Albany
Ph: 09 415 9515

Annie's Wine Bar & Restaurant
Fine Arts Centre, Christchurch
Ph: 03 365 0566

Barcelona
Ground Floor, Clarendon Towers,
Oxford Tce & Worcester Bld, Christchurch
Ph: 03 377 2100

Big Time Café
55 Birkenhead Avenue, Birkenhead
Ph: 09 480 2301

Café Ujazi
28 Tennyson Street, Napier
Ph: 06 835 1490

Food for Life Café
153 Ponsonby Road, Ponsonby
Ph: 09 376 5878

Lusia's Café
523 Great North Road, Grey Lynn
Ph: 09 376 6521

Merlot Wine Café
23 O'Connell Street, Auckland
Ph: 09 309 5456

Musical Knives Restaurant
272 Ponsonby Road, Ponsonby
Ph: 09 376 7354

Nautilus Restaurant
Gulf Harbour Village, Whangaparaoa
Ph: 09 424 3549

Nor'wester Café & Bar
95 Main North Road, Amberley,
North Canterbury
Ph: 03 314 9411

Saint Clair Cellar Door & Café
Cnr Selmes & Rapaura Roads, RD Blenheim
Ph: 03 570 5280

Schwarzwald Konditorei
136 Quay Street, Auckland
Ph: 09 379 6338

Sheraton Hotel
83 Symonds Street, Auckland
Ph: 09 379 5132

St Arnou Brewery & Restaurant
43 Ponsonby Road, Ponsonby
Ph: 09 376 6373

The Old Winery Café
Huangarua Road, Martinborough
Ph: 06 306 8333

The Smokehouse
Shed 3, Mapua Wharf, Nelson
Ph: 03 540 2280

Timara Lodge
Dog Point Road, RD2, Blenheim
Ph: 03 572 8276

Toads Landing
Homebush, Masterton
Ph: 06 377 3793

Vidal Restaurant
913 St Aubyn Street East, Hastings
Ph: 06 876 8105

Contents

What is New Zealand cuisine?

It used to be a common question, and most people thought the answer revolved around meat and three veg, with pavlova to follow. That was pretty simplistic, but it was probably basically accurate – 30 or so years ago.

How things have changed! Imagine asking a room full of people from that time how many had enjoyed either pasta or an Asian meal in the previous week, and posing the same question today. Puts it into perspective, doesn't it?

New Zealand does have a style of cuisine, but it has evolved in an evolutionary rather than a revolutionary fashion. The narrowness of our triple-isled antipodean paradise means no-one lives far from the sea, so it is only right and proper that seafood is playing an increasingly important role in our diet.

In the last few years we have welcomed thousands of Asian immigrants to our country, and they have added their influence to our cuisine.

It is restaurant chefs who have led the change in our eating habits. Many have worked in Mediterranean countries, and they have realised that the same dishes that work in places like Italy, Spain and Greece are perfect for New Zealand conditions. But the best New Zealand recipes aren't copies. Certainly they might incorporate strong influences from the Mediterranean, but they take a strong sideways glance towards Asia, accurately reflecting the changing face of our population.

Strangely, Maori food has had little influence on our national cuisine, but the kumara – a traditional staple – is featured in several dishes in this book, and a couple also make use of Maori bread.

It is to the chefs of the nation that we turned when we sourced our recipes. Ever inventive, and enthusiastic about the produce of their particular region, they have contributed a widely varied collection. Some are more difficult, and will be tackled by only adventurous home cooks, but many others are temptingly simple.

Ian Baker has captured the essence of New Zealand's culinary scene with his superb photographs, and the team that brought you the hugely successful *New Zealand Food, Wine & Art* has created this splendid book.

This is much more than a recipe book – it not only increases our awareness of the culinary riches of our clean, green land, but shouts to the world about the wonderments we have to offer.

Cheers!

Vic Williams

Starters

First-course ideas to bring excitement
to the dining table

Vichyssoise
with Smoked Fish

4 cups chicken stock
4 cups water
75g unsalted butter
3 leeks, white part only, thinly sliced
2 medium onions, peeled and thinly sliced
2 medium potatoes, peeled and thinly sliced
³/₄ cup cream
salt and freshly ground white pepper
150g smoked fish, flaked
1¹/₂ cups mixed milk and water
chopped chives

Put the stock and water on to boil.

Melt the butter in a heavy-based saucepan and in it cook the leek and onion until they are soft, but not at

all brown. Add the potato, stir briefly, then pour the boiling chicken stock and water over. Bring back to the boil and continue cooking for 5 minutes.

Add the cream and cook for a further 2 minutes. Blend in a food processor or blender, then pass through a fine sieve. Return to the pan, adjust the seasoning and keep warm.

Gently poach the smoked fish in the milk and water mixture for 3–4 minutes.

To serve:
Pour the soup into heated bowls, divide the smoked fish between them and garnish with chopped chives.

Serves 4
TIMARA LODGE, BLENHEIM

Rabbit and Basil Ravioli

2 tablespoons olive oil
200g rabbit meat, minced
2 shallots, finely chopped
2 cloves garlic, peeled, crushed and finely chopped
100ml cream
50g raisins
2 tablespoons fresh basil, torn
1 tablespoon fresh thyme, stripped from stalks and chopped
50g redcurrant jelly
salt and pepper

Heat the olive oil in a heavy-based frypan, add the rabbit meat, shallots and garlic and cook, stirring regularly, until the shallots are softened but not coloured and the rabbit is cooked.

Add the cream, raisins, herbs, redcurrant jelly and seasoning and reduce until the liquid has almost evaporated. Check seasoning and put aside to cool.

Smoked Tomato Jus
2 tomatoes
manuka chips
tea from 1 Red Zinger tea bag
1 cup liquid beef stock (venison glaze is used at Annie's)
salt and pepper
100g parmesan cheese

Smoke tomatoes over manuka chips and tea, using a fish smoker. Alternatively, place the manuka chips and tea in a wok and place the tomatoes above on a cake rack, cover with lid but place wet tea towels around the edge to prevent smoke from escaping. Heat for 3–4 minutes until tomatoes are lightly smoked. (Ideally take outside to remove lid because the smoke can be very pervasive!)

Purée in a food processor, put in a saucepan, add seasoning and heat with the beef stock. Check seasoning and keep warm.

Pasta Dough
Round Asian pastry wraps (available at Asian food stores)
1 egg, beaten

Place one heaped teaspoon of filling on a wrapper, brush the edges with beaten egg and place another wrapper on top. Press the edges to seal.

To serve:
Rocket or other green leaves
Flat leaf parsley to garnish

Bring water to a simmer in a shallow pan and poach the ravioli until cooked (approximately 2 minutes). Place leaves on plates, arrange ravioli on top, drizzle with smoked tomato jus and garnish with shaved parmesan cheese and flat leaf parsley.

Serves 4–6

ANNIE'S WINE BAR AND RESTAURANT, CHRISTCHURCH

Takakau

with Green Pea Spread

Takakau (Maori flat bread)
2 cups plain unbleached flour
pinch of salt
pinch of sugar
water to mix

Place the flour, salt and sugar in a large bowl. Drizzle in warm water, mixing with a knife until a dough starts to form. Remove from the bowl and knead on a floured surface until a smooth, elastic ball is formed. Leave to rest under a damp tea towel for at least 10 minutes.

Roll out four discs 20–30cm in diameter and 5mm thick. Place on a floured tray and prick all over with a fork. Bake in a 220°C oven until crisp and brown. Remove, and rest briefly under a clean tea towel.

Spread
3 tablespoons olive oil
1 medium onion, peeled and chopped
1 clove garlic, peeled, crushed and chopped
1 1/2 cups frozen peas, thawed
sea salt and cracked pepper

Heat half the oil and cook the onion and garlic until soft but not at all brown. Add the peas and cook until soft (2–3 minutes). Stir in the remaining olive oil and season to taste. Blend until smooth in a blender or food processor, or make a chunkier version using a mortar and pestle.

To serve:
Cut or tear the warm takakau rounds into chunks and arrange on a platter, with the spread in a bowl alongside.

Serves 4 generously

MERLOT WINE CAFÉ, AUCKLAND

Organic Vietnamese Peanut Butter Soup

4 tablespoons soy or other light vegetable oil
2 medium onions, peeled and diced (reserve the skin)
1 carrot, scrubbed, peeled and diced (reserve the peel)
2 stalks celery, peeled and diced (reserve the peel)
1 tablespoon garlic purée, or 2 cloves garlic, peeled, crushed and chopped
1 tablespoon ginger purée, or 1cm piece ginger, peeled and finely chopped
1 teaspoon chilli paste, or to taste
1 tablespoon ground cumin
1 tablespoon ground coriander
1 teaspoon ground fennel seeds
2–3 cups vegetable stock (recipe below)
400g organic crunchy peanut butter
¹/₂ cup light soy sauce
¹/₂ cup fresh chopped Vietnamese mint (preferably) or coriander, plus whole leaves for garnish
sea salt to taste
sweet soy sauce and coconut flakes, for serving

Vegetable Stock
Reserved vegetable peels, skins and trimmings
4 bay leaves

To make the stock, put the reserved vegetable peels, skins and trimmings and bay leaves in a saucepan with 2¹/₂ litres of water, bring to the boil and simmer for 5 minutes. Strain out and discard the solids. Leftover stock can be refrigerated for up to 3 days, or frozen for up to 3 months.

Heat the oil in a large pot and add the onion, carrot, celery, garlic, ginger, chilli paste, cumin, coriander and fennel. Mix with a wooden spoon until onions are transparent, but not at all brown. Add two cups of vegetable stock and slowly whisk in the peanut butter until the mixture is thick and smooth. Whisk in more stock, and stop when the soup reaches the consistency of thick custard. Add the light soy sauce, Vietnamese mint or fresh coriander and sea salt to taste. Serve garnished with Vietnamese mint, with sweet soy sauce and coconut flakes on the side.

Serves 10–12

MUSICAL KNIVES, AUCKLAND

Gourmet Bread with Avocado/Yoghurt Dip, Dukkah and Basil Pesto

Avocado/Yoghurt Dip
1 cup natural yoghurt
3 tablespoons avocado oil

Place yoghurt in a serving bowl and carefully pool avocado oil over the top.

Basil Pesto
200g fresh basil leaves
100g pine nuts
2 cloves garlic, peeled
50g parmesan cheese
75ml olive oil
pinch of salt

Place all ingredients except salt in a food processor and pulse until mixture is combined, but still chunky. Season to taste and place in a serving bowl.

To serve:
Tear or cut a selection of breads – baguette, panini, rye, bagels, sourdough, sunflower seed, etc. – into interesting shapes and place on a platter with the bowls of avocado/yoghurt dip and basil pesto. Serve a bowl of dukkah alongside.

Serves any number, depending on how much bread you use

Dukkah
4 tablespoons sesame seeds
$1/_3$ cup raw unsalted cashews
$1/_3$ cup almonds
$1/_3$ cup pistachios
3 teaspoons coriander seeds
3 teaspoons cumin seeds

Place all ingredients on a roasting tray and cook in a 180°C oven until light golden. Watch them carefully – they don't take long, and they burn easily.
  Remove from the oven and cool to room temperature. Chop by hand or in a food processor, but leave quite chunky.

Alternative serving suggestion:
extra virgin olive oil
assorted breads

Place the dukkah in a bowl, and the olive oil in another bowl alongside. Tear or cut the bread into chunks. Each guest dips the bread into the oil, then in the dukkah.

Serves 4 generously

NAUTILUS RESTAURANT, AUCKLAND

Fresh Seafood Chowder with Greenshell™ Mussels and Focaccia Croutons

28 fresh greenshell™ mussels
$^1/_2$ cup dry white wine
2 tablespoons unsalted butter
1 medium onion, peeled and chopped
2 cloves garlic, peeled, crushed and chopped
1 stalk celery, peeled and chopped
1 leek, white part only, cleaned thoroughly and chopped
2 cups fish stock
200g tuatua meat, roughly chopped
12 fresh cockles
1 medium potato, peeled and diced
$^1/_4$ cup cream
$^1/_2$ loaf focaccia bread
1 tablespoon olive oil
1 fillet white-fleshed fish (tarakihi, gurnard, snapper, etc.)
1 tablespoon chopped flat leaf parsley

Place the mussels in a wok or pan with the wine, cover and steam until they open. Squeeze together to pull out the beard, then put aside. Strain the cooking liquid and reserve.

Melt half the butter in a heavy-based saucepan and in it cook the onion, garlic, celery and leek until soft but not brown. Add the fish stock and reserved mussel liquid, the tuatua meat and the cockles and bring to the boil. Add the potato and cook until it breaks up and begins to thicken the soup. Remove the cockles (they can be shelled and the meat returned if you like, but watch out for sand).

Purée the soup in a food processor or blender and strain back into the pan. Add the cream and bring back to the boil.

Cut the focaccia into 1cm cubes and fry in the olive oil until lightly browned and crisp. Keep warm.

Cut the fish fillet into 2cm cubes and fry in the remaining butter. Add to the soup.

To serve:
Ladle the soup into four well-heated bowls, garnish with the cooked mussels, focaccia croutons and chopped parsley.

Serves 4

Sheraton Hotel, Auckland

Beer

The rise and rise of the microbrewery

Beer has always played an important part in the New Zealand lifestyle.

Not too many years ago, most good Kiwi blokes got their weekly (or daily) fix from a large glass jug. And we say blokes advisedly – beer was certainly not a drink for women.

But the scene is changing. Microbreweries are popping up all over the country, and their products are commanding huge interest.

In a nutshell, we're drinking less, but drinking better. The modern beer enthusiast will fiercely defend his or her favourite brew, and is quite likely to be seen discussing its merits in a way once reserved for wine *aficionados*.

And there has been another change. Wine had long been considered the only beverage that could be enjoyed as part of a meal, but more and more brewers are making products that are perfect alongside specific dishes. Often, the beer forms part of the dish, making a glass of the same product an obvious and symbiotic accompaniment.

Expect to see more glasses of the brown stuff on the tables of smart restaurants. Beer has been around in this country for a very long time, but in the new millennium it is carving out a whole new niche for itself.

Left: *Guinness is world famous, but in modern New Zealand dozens of purely local names command a big following. Some are available only from the brewhouse where they are made, but others are building a nationwide reputation.*

Right: *Brewing at St Arnou, a popular Auckland boutique brewery.*

Above: *Auckland's Loaded Hog –
beer on the waterfront.*

Beer in Food

New uses for an old favourite

Chicken Pie with Spinach and Pickled Ginger

3 tablespoons vegetable oil
1 medium carrot, peeled and diced
1 medium leek, white part only, thinly sliced
1 large onion, peeled and diced
25g pickled ginger, thinly sliced
2 cloves garlic, peeled, crushed and chopped
1 bay leaf
2 large skinless chicken breasts (approx 500g), diced
200ml dry white wine
500ml chicken velouté sauce (see below)
salt and pepper

Heat the oil in a heavy-based frypan and cook the carrot, leek, onion, ginger, garlic and bay leaf for about 5 minutes, until soft but not brown. Add the chicken and cook until it has turned uniformly white, then stir in the white wine. As soon as the bubbles subside, stir in the velouté and season. Simmer for approximately 5 minutes, or until the chicken is cooked. Reserve, stirring occasionally while it cools.

Velouté Sauce

2 tablespoons butter
4 tablespoons plain flour
3 cups chicken or vegetable stock
salt and pepper
1 teaspoon chopped parsley

Melt the butter in a saucepan. Add the flour and stir over low heat until it just starts to turn golden. Bring the stock to the boil while you are stirring, then add it gradually to the mixture, stirring vigorously with a wire whisk. Add a little salt and pepper and the parsley, and simmer for 30 minutes to 1 hour, until it reaches the consistency of thick cream. Strain through a fine sieve and adjust the seasoning.

Topping

6 thick slices white bread
200ml beer, preferably St Arnou Charlemagne
2 eggs
25g grated parmesan cheese
1 tablespoon chopped parsley
salt and pepper

Cut the bread into triangles or cubes. Combine the beer, eggs, parmesan cheese, parsley and a little salt and pepper, mixing with a fork.

To complete and serve:
150g spinach, washed, blanched in boiling salted water and squeezed dry

Mix the spinach into the chicken mixture and check the seasoning. Divide the filling between four pie dishes. Dip the bread triangles into the beer and egg mixture and arrange over the top, completely covering the filling. Place on a baking sheet and cook in a 200°C oven for 15–20 minutes. Serve with St Arnou Charlemagne beer.

Serves 4

ST ARNOU BREWERY RESTAURANT, AUCKLAND

The St Cloud
Seafood Platter

Marinade for Prawns
1 tablespoon chopped coriander
1 small red chilli, deseeded and chopped
1 clove garlic, peeled and finely chopped
1 lime
4 tablespoons olive oil
salt and pepper

Mix coriander, chilli and garlic. Zest the lime and add this and the juice, then stir in the olive oil. Add salt and pepper to taste.

Salsa
1 small red onion, peeled and finely diced
1 yellow pepper (capsicum), finely diced
1/2 telegraph cucumber, peeled, deseeded and finely diced
1 small red chilli, deseeded and finely chopped
4 leaves fresh basil, torn
8 sprigs curly parsley, finely chopped
salt and pepper
2 tablespoons extra virgin olive oil
2 tablespoons dry white wine
1 tablespoon lemon juice

Mix onion, pepper, cucumber, chilli, basil and parsley, add seasoning to taste, then stir in oil, wine and lemon juice. Allow to stand for 30 minutes before using.

Seafood Mix
16 green prawns
16 greenshell™ mussels
1/2 cup dry white wine
1/2 small red onion, peeled and chopped
2 sprigs parsley, roughly chopped
16 Pacific oysters on the half-shell
cracked pepper
1 tablespoon olive oil
16 prepared baby squid tubes
1 clove garlic, peeled and crushed
1 small red chilli, deseeded and chopped

To complete and serve:
Remove and discard the prawn heads and shells. Cut along the back and remove the grey/green intestinal tract. Toss the tails in the marinade for 30 minutes, then pan-fry or grill until just cooked (2–3 minutes). Thread onto skewers and arrange on a large platter.

Steam the mussels open in the wine with the chopped onion and parsley. Squeeze the shells together to pull off the seaweedy beard, then remove and discard the top shells. Cover the mussels in the bottom shell with the salsa and place on the platter.

The Pacific oysters can be placed on the platter as they are, sprinkled with cracked pepper, or they can be coated with Hollandaise sauce and quickly grilled.

Heat the olive oil in a heavy-based frypan and add the squid tubes, garlic and chilli. Cook just until the squid puffs up and turns opaque (30 seconds to 1 minute). Arrange on the platter. Serve with St Arnou St Cloud beer.

Serves 4 generously

ST ARNOU BREWERY RESTAURANT, AUCKLAND

Wild and Mild Mushroom Soup

100g dried shiitake or Japanese mushrooms (available at Asian food stores)
1 cup hot water
2 tablespoons vegetable oil
1 large white onion, peeled and finely chopped
1–2 leeks, white part only, thinly sliced
2 stalks celery, peeled and chopped
1 clove garlic, peeled, crushed and chopped
4–5 large flat mushrooms (about 200g)
1 medium potato (about 150g), peeled and diced
1 litre vegetable stock
300ml ale, preferably St Arnou Kildara
leaves from 2 sprigs thyme, chopped
salt and pepper
200ml cream

Soak the dried mushrooms in hot water for an hour. Remove and discard the stalks and cut the caps into strips. Strain the water and reserve.

Heat the oil in a deep saucepan and cook the onion, leeks, celery and garlic until soft but not coloured. Cut off and discard most of the stalk from the fresh flat mushrooms, wipe the caps with a damp cloth and slice thickly. Add to the onion mixture, along with half the dried mushrooms. Cook, stirring, for 1 minute, then add the potato, the stock, the reserved mushroom soaking liquid and the ale. Bring to the boil, reduce the heat and simmer for 10 minutes, then add the thyme, plus salt and pepper to taste. Continue to cook for another 15–20 minutes until the potato is soft but hasn't disintegrated. Purée in a blender or food processor, return to the heat and stir in the cream.

To serve:
Check the seasoning, divide among four bowls and top with the reserved shiitake mushrooms. Serve with St Arnou Kildara Ale.

Serves 4

St Arnou Brewery Restaurant, Auckland

Seafood

Fresh from our lakes and seas

N ew Zealanders are lucky. The country is long and narrow, and that means no-one lives more than a few hours from the sea. For seafood lovers, this is paradise.

Given this geographic bonus, it is surprising that meat still forms such a major part of the local diet. Things are changing, but for many people fish is on the menu only once a week, and there are still too many restaurants that include only one or two dishes of the piscatorial persuasion on their menus.

Yet the two food items that inspire more seasonal excitement than any other are both from the sea. Bluff oysters, closely related to the much-revered French Belon, and whitebait, the infant form of up to 11 different fish species, command big money when they first appear each year, but that doesn't stop people from queuing for them.

Far less pricey are New Zealand's unique greenshell™ mussels. Farmed in pristine surroundings in both the North and South Islands, they are delicious. Tuatua and pipis, both in the clam family, are commonly minced and turned into fritters, and their tiny relations, cockles, often play a role in boosting the flavour of chowders and broths. Another clam-like shellfish, the toheroa, is so rare that in most years gathering it is against the law.

Crayfish, known in other parts of the world as rock lobster, are at the upper end of the price scale, but our exchange rate makes them a realistic treat for visitors from Asia and the US. Many restaurants offer diners the opportunity to choose their own 'beast' from a tank. Thankfully, the necessary despatching is done out of sight in the kitchen!

Many of the white-fleshed fish species sold in New Zealand are unique to the local region, but most have equivalents elsewhere. A good fish retailer should be able to give the right advice about choosing a particular type of fish for a specific recipe.

Top left: *Baby farmed paua.*

Above: *The busy fishing port of Napier in Hawke's Bay.*

Right: *A Quinnat salmon, organically farmed in Marlborough's Wairau Valley.*

Far right: *New Zealand's unique greenshell™ mussels.*

Left*: Catch of the day, a champion snapper.*

Seafood

Healthy, delicious and supremely versatile

Oka

400g snapper fillet
zest and juice of 3 lemons
2 tomatoes, deseeded and diced
$^1/_2$ cucumber, peeled, deseeded and diced
$^1/_2$ medium onion, peeled and finely chopped
400g coconut cream
salt and pepper
1 small red chilli, deseeded and chopped (optional)

Cut the fish into 2cm cubes. Add the zest and juice of
the lemons, stir and refrigerate for at least 30 minutes.
   Drain the fish. Add the tomatoes, cucumber and onion,
stir to mix, then stir in the coconut cream.

To serve:
Add seasoning and chopped chilli to taste, then serve
on small plates or in bowls.

LUSIA'S CAFÉ, AUCKLAND

Yellowfin Tuna

with Mussel and Pipi Broth, Wilted Cress and Peruperu Potatoes

Broth

16 small peruperu potatoes,* scrubbed but unpeeled
8 greenshell™ mussels
8 pipis
50g butter
salt and pepper

Tuna

1 tablespoon butter
2 tablespoons olive oil
4 x 150–180g pieces fresh yellowfin tuna
salt and pepper

Place the potatoes in boiling salted water and cook until just tender. Keep warm.

Open the shellfish, either by heating in a microwave or steaming in a little water or dry white wine. Strain the cooking liquid through muslin or a very fine strainer. Put the shellfish and liquid into a pan. Add the butter and a little salt and pepper, then cook for a minute or so, stirring, just until the butter melts and forms an emulsion.

Heat the butter and oil and sear the tuna for a few seconds on each side, then cover loosely with foil and place somewhere warm. It should be rare but warmed through.

To serve:
1 bunch watercress, washed
1/2 lemon

Tear the leaves from the watercress and add to the shellfish broth. As soon as they wilt slightly, drizzle the broth over the bottom of four heated serving bowls. Add the potatoes and arrange the tuna on top. Squeeze the lemon over the fish and serve.

Serves 4

Merlot Wine Café, Auckland

* Peruperu potatoes are often called Maori potatoes, but were actually introduced by Peruvian sailors in the 1800s. They come in several different types, but they all share an earthy flavour and waxy texture.

Prosciutto-wrapped
Salmon on an Artichoke and Beetroot Salad
with Verjuice Dressing and Salsa Verde

Salsa Verde

2 tablespoons capers, preferably salt-packed
1 anchovy, preferably oil-packed
2 tablespoons chopped flat leaf parsley
2 tablespoons chopped mint
1 tablespoon chopped oregano
1 tablespoon peeled and chopped red onion
2 tablespoons extra virgin olive oil
zest of $^1/_2$ a lemon
sea salt (if needed) and cracked pepper

Soak the capers and anchovy in cold water for 30 minutes, remove and chop the anchovy.

Stir all ingredients together until well mixed. Season with cracked pepper. Whether or not you need to add sea salt will depend on the saltiness of anchovies and capers.

Verjuice Dressing

$^1/_4$ cup red wine verjuice
$^1/_4$ cup extra virgin olive oil
pinch of sugar
pinch of sea salt
pinch of cracked pepper

Whisk all ingredients together, using a balloon whisk or fork, until completely combined.

Salad

4 leaves radicchio
sea salt and cracked pepper
1 tablespoon extra virgin olive oil
60g peeled raw beetroot, very thinly sliced
60g raw Jerusalem artichokes, scrubbed and very thinly sliced
1–2 globe artichokes, canned in oil or freshly prepared, halved

Wash and dry the radicchio leaves, brush with olive oil, season and grill until they begin to wilt and brown slightly. Reserve.

Salmon

4 slices prosciutto
4 pieces boneless salmon fillets, approximately 120g each
4 toothpicks
sea salt and cracked pepper
1 tablespoon olive oil

Wrap a slice of prosciutto around each piece of salmon and secure with a toothpick. Season very lightly (the prosciutto will be salty).

Heat the oil in a heavy-based frypan and sear each piece of salmon.

Finish in a 180°C oven for 2–3 minutes (the salmon should be medium-rare).

To serve:
Place a radicchio leaf in the centre of each plate. Toss the vegetables in the verjuice dressing and pile into the leaves. Place a piece of salmon on top of each salad, then drizzle with salsa verde and verjuice dressing.

Serves 4

VIDAL RESTAURANT, HASTINGS

Bluff Oysters
with Chilli, Soy and Lemon Dressing

1 tablespoon Dijon mustard
2 tablespoons white wine vinegar
$1/2$ cup safflower oil (or similar)
1 small red chilli, deseeded and finely chopped
2 teaspoons light soy sauce
2 tablespoons fresh lemon juice
1 clove garlic, peeled, crushed and finely chopped
1 teaspoon finely chopped chervil

24 Bluff oysters, and oyster shells

Whisk all ingredients except the oysters together with a balloon whisk until they emulsify.

To serve:
Pass the oysters through the dressing, using a slotted spoon, then arrange in the shells. Serve on a bed of ice, accompanied by a pile of lightly buttered grainy bread.

Serves 4

SHERATON HOTEL, AUCKLAND

Fish on Prawn Mash

with Baby Leaf Salad, Avocado and Coriander Salsa

6–8 medium potatoes, peeled and quartered
4 tablespoons cream
2 tablespoons butter or olive oil
150g cooked prawn tails, shelled and chopped
salt and pepper
800g skinned and boned firm-fleshed fish, such as kingfish, warehou, bluenose, etc.
25g butter and/or olive oil
1 punnet baby leaf mixed salad, tossed in a dressing made from 1 tablespoon white wine vinegar and 3 tablespoons extra virgin olive oil

Salsa
2 avocados, ripe but quite firm
1 small red pepper (capsicum), diced
2 tomatoes, deseeded and diced
1 small red onion, peeled and finely chopped
50ml lemon juice
50ml extra virgin olive oil
2 tablespoons chopped fresh coriander leaves
salt and pepper

First, make the salsa. Remove the stones from the avocados, scoop out the flesh and dice. Mix with the other ingredients, season to taste and refrigerate until needed.

Boil the potatoes until a piece can be broken with a fork, drain and shake dry over the element. Mash with the cream and butter or olive oil until smooth, then stir in the prawn meat. Add the seasoning and keep warm.

Cut the fish into four serving-sized pieces, pat dry and season. Heat the butter or oil in a heavy-based frypan and seal the fish, then arrange on a baking tray. Cook in a 180°C oven until just cooked (7–10 minutes).

To serve:
Toss the salad with the combined vinegar and olive oil and divide between four plates. Place a scoop of prawn mash in the centre, then arrange a piece of fish over the top. Spoon the salsa over the fish and serve.

Serves 4

THE ALBANY INN, NORTH AUCKLAND

Someone once called New Zealand 'the little green garden at the bottom of the world'.

It was an apt description for a nation where so much emphasis is put on growing things, and where the relatively small population lives in towns separated by thousands of hectares of fields and forests.

Europeans could be forgiven for thinking our country is a mass of kiwifruit vines, such has been the world's acceptance of this furry brown fruit, but there is much more to our horticultural scene than that.

The new crops

One of the most exciting new crops is olives. Pioneered in Marlborough, olives are now grown all over the country, from Northland to Central Otago. The industry has grown enormously since the first trees of modern times were planted in the mid-1980s. A decade later, local olive oil brands could be counted on the fingers of one hand, but by the time the new millennium began, there were enough for leading food and wine magazine, *Cuisine*, to organise a major tasting.

And olive oil isn't the only new product in its field. Locally made avocado oil has a serious following, and one brand combines both avocados and olives. Walnuts have also been used for a local oil that has proved particularly popular with restaurant chefs.

No doubt this is just the beginning. New Zealand horticulturists are an adventurous lot, so the future is bound to feature many new flavour treats.

Avocados and olives – two exciting New Zealand crops. Both have been turned into oil and one enterprising producer has combined the two.

Seared Tasman Bay Scallops

with Roasted Red Pepper and Anchovy Butter on Garlic Crostini

Roasted Red Pepper and Anchovy Butter

5–6 large red peppers (capsicums)
2 tablespoons olive oil
500g butter, well softened
4 anchovy fillets, ideally canned in olive oil
lemon juice to taste
salt and pepper

Cut the peppers in half, remove and discard the stalks, seeds and membranes. Place on an oven tray, skin side down, and drizzle with olive oil. Roast at 190°C until soft. Set two halves aside for garnish, and place a tea towel over the others. Allow to sweat for 15 minutes, then peel.

Place the peeled peppers into a food processor with the butter and anchovies and blend until smooth. Season to taste with lemon juice, salt and pepper. Refrigerate until needed. (This recipe makes much more than you will need, but the remainder can be frozen).

Garlic Crostini

1 baguette or similar French or Italian-style loaf
olive oil
2 cloves garlic
Maldon sea salt and cracked black pepper

Cut the bread on an angle into 1cm-thick slices. Brush with olive oil, place two very thin slivers of garlic on each, season and bake until crisp and golden. Alternatively, bake without garlic, then rub a halved garlic clove over the hot surface.

Scallops

28 scallops, roe on
olive oil
Maldon sea salt and cracked black pepper
25g roasted red pepper and anchovy butter
4 rocket leaves to garnish

Remove and discard the 'boot' from the side of each scallop (look for the ridge of hard flesh opposite the roe). Remove and discard the dark intestinal tract. Heat the oil, and cook the scallops over high heat with a little seasoning for a few seconds on one side – don't overcrowd the pan, or they will poach rather than fry. Turn the scallops over and remove the pan from the heat. Rest for a minute, then swirl the butter into the pan to emulsify with the juices.

To serve:

Place two crostini on each of four heated serving plates, with a quarter of the reserved roasted red peppers on the side. Spoon seven scallops, with a little melted red pepper and anchovy butter, onto each plate and garnish with a rocket leaf.

Serves 4

THE SMOKEHOUSE, MAPUA

Stir-fried Crayfish Omelette

Broth
150ml chicken stock
3 tablespoons Chinese rice wine or dry sherry
1 teaspoon sesame oil
2 tablespoons Vietnamese fish sauce

Omelette
6 large eggs
1 tablespoon palm sugar
1 tablespoon Vietnamese fish sauce
300g crayfish meat, chopped
100g snow pea shoots
3 spring onions, chopped, for garnish
150ml peanut oil
4 tablespoons oyster sauce

Combine all the broth ingredients, bring to the boil and keep warm.

Beat the eggs with the sugar and fish sauce until the sugar dissolves. Combine the crayfish meat, snow pea shoots and chopped spring onion.

Heat the oil in a wok until smoking. Pour in the egg mixture, tipping the wok to ensure a wide coverage. Cook for 2–3 minutes then add the crayfish mixture, placing it in the centre. Cook for a further 3 minutes then remove from the heat. Pour off the oil, fold the omelette and put back on heat for another 1–2 minutes.

To serve:
Place the omelette on a platter and pour warm broth over the top. Top with the oyster sauce and reserved spring onion halves. Cut into four pieces and serve, along with a measure of broth.

Serves 4

TOAD'S LANDING, WAIRARAPA

Steamed Mussels

with Tomatoes and White Wine

4 tablespoons olive oil
40 greenshell™ mussels, scrubbed and beards pulled out
2 cloves garlic, peeled, crushed and chopped
$^1/_2$ cup dry white wine
2 x 400g tins Italian plum tomatoes
salt and freshly ground black pepper
lemon wedges and crusty bread to garnish

Heat the oil in a large saucepan or frypan and add the mussels. Cover and cook for 30 seconds. Add the garlic, cook for 1 minute more, then add the white wine. Reduce by a third, then add the tomatoes, chopped roughly, and some of their juice. Remove from the heat as soon as all the mussels have opened. Season to taste.

To serve:
Remove the mussels with a slotted spoon, discarding any that haven't opened, and divide between four heated serving bowls. Spoon the sauce over the top, and garnish with lemon wedges and bread, plain or lightly toasted.

Serves 4

NAUTILUS RESTAURANT, AUCKLAND

Athene's Special Fish with Greek Salad

Greek Salad

1 tablespoon white wine vinegar
3 tablespoons extra virgin olive oil
sea salt and cracked pepper
1 medium red onion, peeled and chopped
3 tomatoes, deseeded and chopped
10cm piece telegraph cucumber, peeled, deseeded and chopped
1 red and 1 green pepper (capsicum), deseeded and sliced
16 black olives
150g feta cheese

Place vinegar, olive oil and a little salt and pepper in a screw-top jar and shake vigorously to emulsify. Combine all other ingredients with this dressing and check the seasoning.

Tzatziki Dressing

¹/₂ cup Greek-style yoghurt
¹/₂ cup finely chopped mint leaves
1 telegraph cucumber, peeled, deseeded and finely chopped
1 clove garlic, peeled, crushed and finely chopped
sea salt and cracked pepper

Stir all ingredients together until well combined. Check seasoning.

Fish

4 fillets skinned and boned snapper or tarakihi, or 8 fillets gurnard
flour for dusting
salt and pepper
2 tablespoons olive oil

Coat the fish with flour, then season.

Heat the oil in a heavy-based frypan and cook the fish until it is just opaque right through.

To serve:
Place a pile of Greek salad on each of four plates. Place a fillet of fish on top of each pile, then drizzle tzatziki dressing over the top.

Serves 4

CAFÉ UJAZI, NAPIER

Hot-smoked
Tarakihi and Bacon with Potato Dumplings and Creamed Spinach

Creamed Spinach

2 bunches fresh spinach, thick stems removed, or 160g frozen spinach
2 tablespoons olive oil
1 medium onion, peeled and chopped
³/₄ cup cream
salt and pepper

Wilt the spinach by throwing it into a saucepan of boiling salted water for a few seconds, then drain it well and squash to remove excess water.

Heat the oil and cook the onion until it is soft but not at all brown. Add the spinach and cream and cook until reduced a little or, if using frozen spinach, until it has defrosted. Don't cook it so much that it loses its bright green colour. Season to taste.

Potato Dumplings

1kg floury potatoes, scrubbed but unpeeled
2 egg yolks
2 tablespoons parmesan cheese
125–185g plain flour

Prick the potatoes all over, then bake in a 180°C oven for 1 hour, or until tender. Leave to cool for 15 minutes, then peel and mash.

Stir in the egg yolks and parmesan cheese, then gradually sift in the flour. When the mixture gets too dry to use a spoon, work it with your hands. Once a loose dough forms, transfer it to a lightly floured surface and knead gently. Work in enough extra flour to give a soft, pliable dough that is damp to touch, but not sticky.

Divide the dough into six portions. Working with one portion at a time, roll out on the floured surface to form a rope about 1.5cm thick. Cut into 1.5cm lengths. Continue with the remaining dough.

Bring a large saucepan of salted water to the boil and add the dumplings in batches of about 20. Stir gently and return to the boil. Cook for 1–2 minutes, or until they rise to the surface. Remove with a slotted spoon.

To complete and serve:
4 medium-sized tarakihi or other white-fleshed fish fillets, hot-smoked, skinned and boned
8 rashers good quality bacon, grilled slightly crisp

Heat the creamed spinach and divide it between four heated shallow serving bowls. Arrange five dumplings around the edge of each bowl. Warm the tarakihi fillets in the microwave or a little simmering water and break into large pieces. Put a pile of spinach in the centre of each bowl and scatter the tarakihi pieces over the top. Finish with a 'cap' of two bacon rashers.

Serves 4

Note: All the components of this dish can be prepared the day before and reheated. If there is no time to make the dumplings, substitute mashed potato or steamed baby new potatoes.

The Smokehouse, Mapua

Baby Paua in Brandy Cream Sauce on a Whitebait Soufflé

Brandy Cream Sauce
1 tablespoon unsalted butter
3 cloves garlic, peeled, crushed and chopped
3 tablespoons brandy
1 cup fish stock*
$^1/_2$ cup dry white wine
1 cup cream

Melt the butter in a heavy-based pan and cook the garlic for a couple of minutes over low to medium heat. Don't let it brown. Pour in the brandy, stir quickly, then set fire to it (be careful if you have a powerful range hood). When the flames subside, add the fish stock and reduce by two-thirds. Add the wine and reduce again by half, then add the cream and cook until the sauce has attained a good pouring consistency. Keep warm.

* To make fish stock, bring fish bones to the boil in a litre or so of water, add roughly chopped herbs (dill, parsley, etc.) and a chopped onion, then simmer very gently for 20 minutes. Strain through muslin. Leftover stock can be kept for 3 days in the refrigerator, or frozen for up to 3 months.

Baby Paua
4 baby paua
1 tablespoon butter

Remove paua from shell, discard gut and clean carefully to clear of sand and grit. Slice thinly, then sear for a few seconds in the butter. Place back in shell and keep warm.

Whitebait Soufflés
160g West Coast whitebait
4 medium eggs, preferably free-range
100ml cream
2 teaspoons chopped fresh dill
1 teaspoon finely chopped orange zest
sea salt and freshly ground black pepper
butter for greasing moulds

Pick over the whitebait to remove any 'debris' – don't wash.

Whisk together eggs, cream, dill, orange zest and a generous pinch each of salt and pepper, then gently stir in the whitebait.

Rub butter around four egg rings and place in a buttered, heated shallow pan. Add a thin layer of the whitebait mixture to each and heat gently until it sets. Pour in the remaining mixture, then transfer the pan to a 180°C oven. Cook for approximately 8 minutes.

Remove from the oven and lift the soufflés from the pan with an egg slice. Run a sharp knife around the edge of each egg ring to release.

To serve:
1 cup rocket leaves
1 teaspoon extra virgin olive oil
sea salt and cracked black pepper

Wash and thoroughly dry the rocket leaves and remove the stalks. Toss in the oil with a little salt and pepper.

Divide rocket leaves between four warmed plates. Place a whitebait soufflé on each, leaving an indentation in the middle. Pour the brandy cream sauce over the paua in the shells, and place one shell on top of each soufflé. Surround with the remaining sauce.

Serves 4

Sheraton Hotel, Auckland

Whole Roasted Snapper in Foil

2 whole snapper (approx. 27cm long), scaled, gutted and gills removed
salt and pepper to taste
100g butter, softened
zest and juice from 1 lemon and 1 orange
18 baby potatoes, scrubbed and parboiled until almost cooked
several sprigs fresh rosemary

Wash the whole snapper inside and out and wipe dry. Place each one on a piece of foil larger than the fish and season to taste with salt and pepper. Combine the butter with the zest and juice of the lemon and orange, stirring until well mixed, and smear over each fish and inside the cavity. Divide the potatoes between the two fish and place some in the cavities, scattering the rest over the foil. Cut diagonal slits into the flesh and insert sprigs of rosemary.

Place a second piece of foil over each fish and fold the sheets together to form two parcels. Place on a baking sheet and cook in a preheated 180°C oven for 25–30 minutes. Test by unfolding the foil and making sure the flesh flakes easily and the juices run clear. Remove the top sheet of foil and serve the fish with a fresh salad or seasonal vegetables of your choice.

Serves 6

Nautilus Restaurant, Auckland

New Zealand wine

Fresh-faced magic in a glass

Every year, a restaurant in the American city of Boston organises an 'Oysters with Wine' competition. The oysters come from all the US. The wines are from all over the world.

A couple of years ago, New Zealand wines were included for the first time, and they took their place, masked, as part of the 487-bottle line-up. When the judges had made their choices and the labels were revealed, five of the first ten places, including the first, second and third slots, had gone to Marlborough wines made from the sauvignon blanc grape.

It was an extraordinary result, and it gives some idea of the huge world-wide excitement that has been caused by this jump-out-of-the-glass style.

But New Zealand is no one-grape wonder. Marlborough sauvignon has been called 'the first totally new wine style of the last 100 years', but all our wines have a point of difference. People have tried to compare our cabernet sauvignon with Australian examples, and our chardonnays with great white burgundy. That's a mistake. New Zealand wines are unique, partly because they have a flavour intensity shared by few others around the world.

In winemaking terms, we are a cool-climate nation, but we also enjoy long sunshine hours. Local grapes build their flavour strength during the day, and consolidate it through the cool nights. The result is wines with upfront fruit that shouts of its attributes.

It is sauvignon blanc that has put us on the international wine map, but New Zealand also produces elegant riesling, nicely focused chardonnay, velvety merlot and exceedingly stylish pinot noir.

And that is only the major varieties. Gewürztraminer, pinot gris, syrah and a host of others have shown that in the hands of a skilled winemaker, they can produce wines that rival the best in the world.

Top: *Marlborough's Wairau Valley, the most extensively planted grape-growing region in New Zealand.*

Right: *Sampling wine is becoming a popular recreational pastime.*

Poultry

A bird in the hand ... delicious recipes
for chicken and other feathered delights

Supreme of
Asian-style Duck

This recipe can be started a day before.

3 cinnamon quills
7 star anise
8 duck supremes (breast with the bone retained)
$^1/_2$ stalk rosemary
50ml peanut oil

Roast the cinnamon quills and star anise in a 180°C oven until fragrant (about 5 minutes).

Trim any excess fat from the duck and score the skin. Place in a bowl or pan with all ingredients. Turn to coat thoroughly. Refrigerate and marinate for at least an hour, or overnight.

Roast the duck in a 180°C oven until done to your liking (duck breast is good rare or medium rare, as long as it is tender). Keep warm.

Chinese Glaze
2 cinnamon quills
6 star anise
2 cloves
8 juniper berries
500ml beef stock (venison glaze is used at Annie's)
50ml redcurrant jelly

Roast the cinnamon, star anise, cloves and juniper berries in a 180°C oven until fragrant. Stir into the stock or glaze, add redcurrant jelly and reduce until it reaches a good pouring consistency. Keep warm.

Curried Red Lentils
100g red lentils
6 curry leaves
2 tablespoons curry powder

2 garlic cloves, peeled but left whole
2 tablespoons peanut oil
100ml chicken stock
salt and pepper

Wash lentils thoroughly and drain. Pan-fry the curry leaves, curry powder and garlic in the oil for 2–3 minutes, being careful not to let the garlic burn.

Add lentils and stock, and simmer until the lentils are cooked, but still retain a little 'bite'. Season to taste and keep warm.

Asian Vegetables
snow peas
snow pea sprouts
bok choy or choy sum
baby spinach
2 tablespoons peanut oil
2 slices peeled fresh ginger, chopped

Pull the strings from around the edges of the snow peas. Chop all vegetables roughly. Heat the oil and pan-fry the vegetables briefly with the ginger until slightly wilted, but still bright green.

To serve:
Divide the lentils among eight plates, place a pile of vegetables on top, then a duck supreme on top again. Remove and discard the spices from the glaze and pour it over the duck.

Serves 8

ANNIE'S WINE BAR AND RESTAURANT, CHRISTCHURCH

Chargrilled Free-range Chicken with Seared Scallops on Curried Puy Lentils

Curry Sauce

1 tablespoon peanut oil
$^1/_2$ teaspoon Thai green curry paste
1 tablespoon chopped ginger
$^1/_2$ teaspoon turmeric
2 kaffir lime leaves
1 stalk lemongrass, centre part only, finely chopped
1 tablespoon brown sugar
1 clove garlic, peeled, crushed and chopped
1 tablespoon lime juice
2 tablespoons fish sauce
4 cups coconut cream

Heat peanut oil in a heavy-based frypan or saucepan at medium temperature.

Add all dry ingredients except sugar and garlic. Cook, stirring, until softened but not at all coloured. Add garlic and sugar, stir, then add all liquid ingredients. Give a final stir, then simmer for 5 minutes. Remove and discard kaffir lime leaves and turn off heat. Check seasoning, adding salt if necessary, and reserve.

Lentils

1 cup puy lentils
1 teaspoon sea salt

Pick over the lentils, discarding any 'debris', then wash thoroughly in cold water (there is no need to soak puy lentils).

Bring three cups of water to the boil in a large saucepan, add salt, then trickle in the lentils. Simmer for 25 minutes, drain thoroughly and reserve.

Chicken

2 double skinless chicken breasts
1 tablespoon peanut oil
sea salt and freshly ground black pepper

Cut the double breasts into singles, and trim off any fat or gristle. Pull or cut out the white wedge-ended tendon that runs the length of each fillet and remove, to prevent curling. Brush the breasts with oil, then season.

Cook in a 180°C oven until just cooked through (15–20 minutes). Remove and allow to rest.

Scallops

12 scallops, including roe
2 tablespoons peanut oil
sea salt and cracked pepper

Trim the hard 'boot' from one side of the scallops (it can be seen as a slightly firmer piece of flesh, usually opposite the orange roe), and the dark intestinal vein from the other. Discard.

Heat the oil in a heavy-based frypan at high temperature.

Sear scallops for about 30 seconds on each side, or until they are just opaque right through. Season lightly.

To serve:
1 tablespoon chopped coriander leaves or torn spinach leaves

Reheat the curry sauce and add the cooked lentils. Stir in the coriander or spinach and cook just until wilted.

Place a generous spoonful of the lentil mixture in the centre of each of four shallow preheated bowls.

Place one chicken breast on top of each pile, and arrange three scallops around the edge of each bowl. At Vidal Restaurant, the dish is garnished with a whole Anaheim pepper, dipped in beaten egg and cornmeal (polenta) and shallow fried.

Serves 4

VIDAL RESTAURANT, HASTINGS

Chargrilled Chicken with Spicy Penne Pasta

6 boneless chicken thighs, skin removed
salt and pepper
6 tablespoons olive oil
500g penne pasta
3 Spanish-style chorizo sausages, sliced
1 red pepper (capsicum), diced
1 clove garlic, peeled, crushed and chopped
$^1/_2$ cup dry white wine
200g spinach leaves, thick stalks removed
3 tablespoons chopped parsley
3 tablespoons shaved or grated parmesan cheese

Season the chicken and barbecue, grill or pan-fry, using two tablespoons of the olive oil. Cook the penne pasta in three litres of salted boiling water according to the packet directions. Drain and toss with a little oil to prevent it from sticking together.

While the pasta is cooking, heat two tablespoons of olive oil in a heavy-based frypan and cook the chorizo, pepper and garlic until soft, then add the wine. Simmer until reduced by half. Roughly chop the spinach and toss through, then add the reserved penne. Check the seasoning.

To serve:
Divide the penne mixture between four heated serving bowls, cut the chicken into strips and arrange over the top. Garnish with the parsley and parmesan cheese.

THE ALBANY INN, NORTH AUCKLAND

Asian Chicken

Chicken
160g dried figs
30g pickled ginger
¹/₂ spring onion, chopped
salt and pepper
chicken thighs

Place figs, ginger and spring onion in a food processor and blend briefly to a chunky consistency (not a paste). Season to taste. Stuff the mixture under the skin of each chicken thigh and use toothpicks to secure the skin back into its original position and seal the join. Season lightly and roast in a 180°C oven for 7–10 minutes.

Steamed Asian-style Vegetables
baby bok choy, broken into individual leaves
Chinese cabbage, roughly chopped
daikon radish, peeled and cut into strips lengthways
carrots, peeled and shaved lengthways into ribbons

Steam or blanch in salted water for 1 minute, until cooked but still crisp.

Cashew Nut Sauce
30ml canola oil
3 shallots, peeled and diced
1 clove garlic, peeled and finely chopped
50g fresh ginger, peeled and chopped
1 small hot red chilli, deseeded and chopped
¹/₂ red pepper (capsicum), deseeded and diced
1 teaspoon ground cumin
300ml coconut cream
200ml fresh cream
250g cashew nuts, roasted but unsalted
30g brown sugar
1 stalk lemongrass, centre part only
20ml lemon juice
salt and pepper
handful coriander leaves, some left whole, some finely chopped

Heat the oil in a heavy-based pan and gently fry the shallots, garlic, ginger, chilli, pepper and cumin until they are soft but not coloured. Add the remaining ingredients except the coriander leaves, bring to the boil, stirring, then reduce heat and simmer for 5 minutes. Remove from heat, allow to cool slightly, then blend in a food processor to a smooth sauce consistency. Season to taste and garnish with the chopped coriander.

Wild Rice Roll
3 tablespoons butter
100g shiitake mushrooms
150g flat mushrooms
200g wild rice, cooked
1 spring onion, finely diced
¹/₂ red pepper (capsicum), deseeded and finely diced
salt and pepper
8 spring roll wrappers (available in Asian food stores)
white of 1 egg, lightly beaten
1 litre peanut or canola oil

Heat the butter in a heavy-based frypan and cook the mushrooms. Allow to cool slightly, then dice. Mix with the wild rice, add the spring onion and red pepper and season to taste.

Place a spring roll wrapper on the bench with one corner facing you. Place a quarter of the wild rice mixture in the middle. Brush the edges with egg white, then fold the bottom point over the mixture. Fold in the side points, sealing the filling in, then follow through with the bottom edge to complete the roll. Place on another wrapper and repeat the process, forming a double layer. When you have four rolls, they can be deep-fried in peanut or canola oil for approximately 4 minutes, or until golden brown.

To serve:
Divide the cashew nut sauce between four preheated shallow bowls. Arrange some of the Asian vegetables on top, then place a roasted chicken thigh, cut on the diagonal to show the filling, on top of each pile of vegetables. Lean a spring roll, also cut diagonally to show the filling, against each chicken thigh. Garnish with whole coriander leaves.

Serves 4

Nor'wester Café and Bar, Waipara

Meat

The product of a clean, green land

Meat has always played a big part in the New Zealand diet. Inevitably, in a country where sheep outnumber people by something like twenty to one, lamb and mutton have traditionally occupied pride of place, but beef has also made a major contribution over the years. Pork was once considered a special-occasion treat, but that has changed. Now, it appears regularly on most shopping lists.

More exotic fare is restricted mainly to restaurants. Cervena™ (farmed venison) can be ordered by most butchers or purchased by mail order, but is still seen on few home dining tables. Ostrich and emu, also farmed here, are rare even in restaurants – strangely, diners are more likely to encounter kangaroo from Australia.

The clichéd Kiwi meal has long been cited as 'meat and three veg'. Potatoes were always included, usually accompanied by something green and something orange, but meat was the major player.

The influence of Mediterranean and Asian cultures has changed the emphasis. Many Asian dishes and pasta recipes use only small amounts of meat, and many people make a point of enjoying one or two completely meatless meals a week.

A few years ago, health fears frightened some people off red meat, but it is now well understood that fat is the culprit. Forward-thinking farmers are breeding leaner animals, and it is a simple matter to trim off any excess fat as the meal is being prepared.

After all, meat is one of the most versatile ingredients we can use. A beef steak, seared in a hot pan, is very different in both taste and texture from a piece of beef shin, cooked for a couple of hours in red wine and stock with aromatic vegetables, yet both come from the same animal. The same applies to other types of meat, and it is the reason that beef, lamb, pork and the exotics will always be an important part of our diet.

Meat, fresh and cured, has been an important earner of export dollars for New Zealand. Our animals spend all year outdoors.

Meat

Starting point for a million meals

Peppers

Stuffed with Feta, Basil and Chorizo Sausages

8 small peppers (capsicums), various colours
4 tablespoons olive oil
4 Spanish-style chorizo sausages, chopped
2 cloves garlic, peeled, crushed and chopped
1 medium onion, peeled and finely chopped
250g feta cheese, crumbled
small handful fresh basil, torn
salt and pepper

Sauce Vierge

150ml olive oil
3 cloves garlic, peeled, crushed and chopped
400g tomatoes, deseeded and chopped
5 tablespoons Balsamic vinegar
$^{1}/_{2}$ cup fresh basil leaves, torn
1 teaspoon sugar
salt and pepper

First, make the sauce. Gently heat the oil, add the garlic and cook until softened but not brown, then stir in the other ingredients. Heat just to warm through and infuse the flavours. Keep warm.

Cut the peppers in half lengthways and remove the ribs and seeds. Heat the oil and cook the sausages, garlic and onion until softened but not coloured. Mix with the feta and basil, season to taste and spoon into the pepper halves. Grill or bake until tender.

To serve:
Divide the sauce vierge among four serving plates and arrange the peppers around the edge.

Serves 4

Toad's Landing, Wairarapa

Blackened Lamb with Pickled Vegetables

1 lamb loin or rump, large enough for four people
2 tablespoons olive oil

Marinade
2 tablespoons coriander seeds
2 tablespoons fennel seeds
1 tablespoon cardamom pods
1 tablespoon black peppercorns
2 teaspoons cumin seeds
1 teaspoon fenugreek seeds
1 teaspoon black mustard seeds
5 cloves
1 cinnamon quill, broken up
2 teaspoons cayenne pepper
1 teaspoon ground ginger

Dry-fry all the whole spices in a heavy-based frypan until they are fragrant, stirring frequently to prevent them from burning. Add the powdered spices at the last minute, then remove and grind them all together, using an old coffee grinder or a mortar and pestle.

Brush the lamb with oil and rub the spice mixture into the meat, pressing it in with your fingers. Refrigerate for at least an hour, or overnight. Any leftover spice mix will keep well in an airtight container.

Sear the lamb on a barbecue or in a very hot frypan (a warning – it smokes!), then lower the heat and cook to medium-rare. It can be finished in a 180°C oven, but the surface should be very dark brown and even black in parts. Cover with foil and put in a warm place to rest.

Pickled Vegetables
2 tablespoons olive oil
4 orange kumara (sweet potatoes), peeled and cut into 2cm dice
300g shallots, peeled but left in bulbs
6 courgettes (zucchini), unpeeled, cut into 2cm dice
2 teaspoons cumin seeds
1¹/₂ teaspoons fenugreek seeds
4 curry leaves, shredded
4 cloves garlic, peeled, crushed and chopped
1 teaspoon sweet chilli sauce
1 tablespoon tomato purée
6 tablespoons white wine vinegar

Heat the oil in a heavy-based pan and fry the vegetables over medium heat until they are just cooked through. Remove and keep warm.

Fry the spices in the residual oil until they are fragrant, add the curry leaves and garlic, stir briefly, then the chilli sauce and tomato purée. Cook for another minute, then add the vinegar. Stir the reserved vegetables into the mix.

Minted Lemon Yoghurt
¹/₂ cup plain yoghurt
rind of one lemon plus 1 teaspoon juice
2 tablespoons chopped mint leaves

Stir all ingredients together.

To serve:
Place a pile of vegetables in the centre of each plate. Slice the lamb, and arrange over the top. Drizzle with minted lemon yoghurt.

Optional:
Garnish with onion rings, dusted with flour and deep-fried.

Serves 4

VIDAL RESTAURANT, HASTINGS

Rewana Special

(served for breakfast)

20 button mushrooms
6 tablespoons butter
$^1/_2$ cup cream
sea salt and cracked pepper
8 rashers lean bacon
8 eggs, preferably free-range
8 slices Maori bread (rewana) or plain white bread
spring onion curls, to garnish

Thinly slice the mushrooms and pan-fry in half the butter. Add the cream and reduce to a good sauce consistency. Season to taste and keep warm.

Grill the bacon until crisp. Keep it warm on paper towels.

Poach the eggs to the soft-yolk stage.

Toast the bread and smear with the remaining butter.

To serve:
Arrange two slices of toast, overlapping, on each of four heated serving plates. Divide the mushrooms among the plates and place two poached eggs and two bacon rashers on each. Garnish with the spring onion.

Serves 4

Café Ujazi, Napier

Rewana Bread

This bread needs to be made in three steps, so allow plenty of time.

Step One: Rewana Starter
3 slices medium potato
2 cups plain flour
1 teaspoon sugar

Boil the potato slices in water to cover until they reach mashing consistency. Cool slightly in the cooking water (don't discard). When lukewarm, add the remaining ingredients and mix to a fairly firm texture, adding more warm water if necessary. Cover and leave to prove in a warm place for 2–3 hours, just as you would for a yeast-based starter.

Step Two: Rewana Dough
5 cups plain flour
1 teaspoon salt
rewana starter
1 teaspoon baking soda

Combine the flour and salt in a large bowl, Make a well in the centre and add the rewana starter. Sprinkle the baking soda over the top.

Add a couple of good splashes of warm water and mix until a dough is formed.

If it is too wet, sprinkle on more flour; if too firm, add more warn water.

Continue to knead on a lightly floured surface for about 10 minutes, or until the dough is smooth and pliable. Cover with a damp cloth and leave to prove in a warm place for an hour.

Step Three: Moulding and Baking
Place the dough on a floured surface and knead lightly. Mould into a loaf shape and place in a lightly oiled bread tin. Cover again with a damp cloth and leave to prove in a warm place for 30 minutes.

Preheat the oven to 160°C and bake for $1^1/_2$–2 hours, or until a skewer can be inserted into the centre and comes out clean.

Merlot Wine Café, Auckland

Cumin-roasted Pork Fillets
with Red Pepper Relish and Spinach on Honey-roasted Kumara

Red Pepper Relish
2 tablespoons olive oil
1 large onion, peeled and sliced
10 red peppers (capsicums), cut into strips
6 cloves garlic, peeled, crushed and chopped
500ml cider vinegar
2 cups raw sugar
1 teaspoon salt
500ml tomato juice

Heat the oil in a non-reactive frypan and cook the onion and peppers until they begin to colour. Add the garlic and cook for another minute, then add the vinegar, sugar and salt. Cook on medium-high until the mixture is reduced by a third (it should be quite syrupy), then stir in the tomato juice and reduce by another third.

Note: This recipe makes up more relish than you will need for the pork dish, but it is a useful store cupboard item, delicious with meat on panini or as part of an antipasto platter, or as a topping for mushroom risotto.

Pork Fillets
2 large pork fillets, trimmed of all sinew and excess fat
250g fresh spinach, well washed, thicker stalks removed
150g Red Pepper Relish (recipe above)

Butterfly the fillets lengthways so they lie flat and open, and spread liberally with the Red Pepper Relish. Place the spinach leaves over the top and roll up to resemble a Swiss roll. Secure with toothpicks or tie with string if necessary. Refrigerate until needed.

Honey-roasted Kumara
1kg golden or orange kumara (sweet potatoes)
2 tablespoons honey
3 cloves garlic, peeled, crushed and chopped
1 tablespoon sesame seeds
1 tablespoon olive oil
salt and pepper

Peel the kumara and quarter lengthways. Place in a baking tray with the other ingredients and toss over a hot element until the honey is melted and everything is well mixed. Roast in a 190°C oven for 20 minutes.

Cumin Crust
25g unsalted butter
2 cloves garlic, peeled, crushed and chopped
1 teaspoon ground cumin
200g breadcrumbs

Heat the butter in a heavy-based frypan and cook the other ingredients until golden. Keep warm.

To complete and serve:
olive oil
stock or white wine

Sear the pork fillets in a hot frypan with a little olive oil, browning on all sides. Transfer to a 200°C oven for 10 minutes, or until just cooked. Deglaze the pan with a little stock or white wine and reduce to a pouring consistency. Divide the honey-roasted kumara between four heated plates, slice the pork on the diagonal and arrange over the top, drizzle with the pan liquid, sprinkle with the cumin crust and serve. Garnish with extra red pepper relish.

Serves 4

BIG TIME CAFÉ, AUCKLAND

Polynesian-style Chop Suey

1 packet vermicelli noodles
2¼ cups water
2 tablespoons soy oil
½ medium onion, peeled and chopped
3 cloves garlic, peeled, crushed and finely chopped
3 slices peeled ginger, finely chopped
400g beef schnitzel, cut into finger-sized strips
2–3 teaspoons dark soy sauce
salt and pepper

Soak the vermicelli noodles in the cold water for 30 minutes, drain, then cut roughly with scissors. Reserve.

Heat the oil and cook the onion, garlic and ginger until soft but not at all brown. Add the beef strips and vermicelli noodles and toss to mix. Cook until the liquid has been reduced by half. Stir in enough soy sauce to achieve a mid-brown colour and cook until all the liquid has been absorbed.

To serve:
Add seasoning to taste and serve in heated bowls or plates.

Serves 4

LUSIA'S, AUCKLAND

Seared Venison Scotch Fillet

on Kumara Penupenu with Fragrant Mushrooms and Grilled Winter Vegetables

4 large kumara (sweet potatoes)
2 carrots
3 large potatoes
2 parsnips
150ml cream
50g butter
salt and pepper
8 flat mushrooms, stem mostly removed, wiped clean
2 tablespoons red wine
vegetables to grill, such as capsicums, pumpkin wedges, halved turnips, etc.
olive oil
4 venison Scotch fillet steaks, approximately 200g each*

Peel kumara, carrots, potatoes and parsnips, cut into chunks and boil. When soft, drain, dry over the element and mash, adding the butter and cream. Season to taste. This is the kumara penupenu.

Season the mushrooms and place in a pan with a cup of water. Simmer until cooked through and the water has reduced, then add the wine. Keep warm.

Parboil the winter vegetables if necessary (it depends on what you choose), brush with olive oil and grill. Alternatively, they can be baked. Keep warm.

Season the venison steaks and cook them in a little olive oil to the degree you prefer (they are best rare). Put in a warm place to rest for a few minutes.

* The Merlot Wine Café uses feral venison.

To serve:
Divide the kumara penupenu between four heated serving plates. Place a venison steak on top of each serving, arrange the mushrooms on top then pour their cooking liquid over everything. Garnish with the grilled winter vegetables.

Serves 4

MERLOT WINE CAFÉ, AUCKLAND

Spiced Lamb Shanks

This recipe can be started a day before.

Marinade
1 teaspoon cumin seeds
1 teaspoon coriander seeds
$^1/_2$ teaspoon fennel seeds
1 star anise
$^1/_2$ cinnamon stick
2 kaffir lime leaves
1 fresh chilli
1 clove garlic, peeled
8 tablespoons olive oil

8 lamb shanks

Casserole Stock
2 carrots
3 stalks celery
2 medium onions, unpeeled
1 whole head garlic
1 lemon
2–3 cups beef stock
2 sprigs rosemary
3 sprigs mint
1 teaspoon tomato paste
salt and pepper

To make the marinade, roast or dry-fry the dry spices until aromatic, watching carefully to prevent burning. Place with the lime leaves, chilli and garlic in a grinder or mortar and pestle and grind to a coarse powder. Mix with half the olive oil to form a paste and rub on the lamb shanks. Refrigerate for at least 2 hours, or overnight.

Preheat a heavy-based frypan, add the remaining oil and cook the shanks, turning frequently, until they are well browned. Transfer to a casserole.

To make the casserole stock, roughly chop the carrots, celery, onions, garlic and lemon and brown in a heavy-based frypan, then add to the casserole with the shanks. Add enough beef stock (or water) to cover, then add the rosemary, mint, tomato paste and salt and pepper. Cover and cook in a 200°C oven for 30 minutes, then reduce heat to 160°C and cook for a further 2$^1/_2$–3$^1/_2$ hours, until very tender.

Remove the shanks with a slotted spoon and keep warm. Strain the vegetables and herbs from the stock and discard. Reduce the cooking liquid over direct heat until it reaches a good sauce consistency, or thicken with cornflour and water if necessary. Check the seasoning.

To serve:
Place mashed potatoes (flavoured, if you like, with crushed chopped cloves of roast garlic and chopped parsley) on four heated plates or shallow bowls. Place two shanks on each pile of potatoes, and cover with the reduced cooking liquid. Accompany with braised vegetables such as carrot and parsley sticks, and baby onions.

Serves 4

NOR'WESTER CAFÉ AND BAR, WAIPARA

Braised Pork Belly with Creamed Mash and Crisp Greens

2–3 kg piece pork belly
$1/4$ cup sweet chilli sauce
$1/4$ cup oyster sauce (both sauces are available at Asian food stores)
4 tablespoons brown sugar
4 potatoes
$1/4$ cup cream
25g butter
salt and pepper
seasonal green vegetable (beans, bok choy, cabbage, etc.)

Place the pork, skin side up, in a large roasting dish. Pour the two sauces over the top, and sprinkle the sugar over. Half fill the dish with water and cover with foil. Bake in a 150°C oven for 3–4 hours, or until the meat is literally 'melt-in-the-mouth' tender.

Peel the potatoes and cut into chunks. Cook in boiling salted water until a piece can be broken apart with a fork. Drain, then dry over heat. Mash with the cream and butter until smooth and season to taste.

Steam or boil your chosen green vegetable until it is just done. Season to taste.

To serve:
Divide the mashed potato between four heated serving plates. Cut the pork into serving chunks and arrange over the top with some of the cooking liquid, Garnish with the green vegetable.

Serves 4

MERLOT WINE CAFÉ, AUCKLAND

One-pan Lamb's Liver and Bacon with Gourmet Mash

1kg waxy potatoes (e.g. Agria or Mondial)
olive oil or butter, for mashing
salt and white pepper
250g good-quality bacon
1 large onion, peeled and thinly sliced
500g lamb's liver, de-veined and cut into
12 medium-thick slices
250ml beef stock
1 teaspoon mint jelly
1 teaspoon sweet chilli sauce (optional)
hot English mustard

Steam or boil the potatoes and mash with olive oil or butter until smooth. Season generously and keep warm.

Use a little butter or olive oil to cook the bacon, and add the onion once the bacon has rendered a little of its fat. Cook until the onions are golden and the bacon crisp. Remove and keep warm. Add more oil or butter to the pan if necessary and cook the liver, turning as soon as it colours on one side. Add the bacon and onions and pour the stock over. Simmer for 2 minutes, season to taste, and stir in the mint jelly and, if using, the sweet chilli sauce. If necessary, remove the major ingredients and keep warm while you reduce the sauce to a good pouring consistency.

To serve:
Divide the mashed potato between four heated plates. Arrange three pieces each of liver and bacon on the potato and spoon the sauce over the top. Serve the mustard on the side. At The Old Winery Café, this dish is often served with Brussels sprouts.

Serves 4

THE OLD WINERY CAFÉ, MARTINBOROUGH

Eating plenty of fruit and vegetables is the easiest way to enjoy the fibre that forms an important part of every healthy diet.

There's plenty of choice. Not too many years ago, the home cook had to select from around half a dozen root vegetables and not many more greens. Exotic species like eggplant and fennel were unheard of, and the only available lettuce was the super-hardy iceberg.

Fruit and vegetables

Making fibre fun

Two things changed all that. Firstly, our restaurant chefs realised our climate was ideally suited to Mediterranean fare, and they began looking to Italy and Spain for their inspiration. Secondly, we opened our doors to migrants from China, Korea, Taiwan and other Asian nations, and demand soon encouraged growers to supply the vegetables they were used to.

Now, the home cook can choose large or baby eggplants, peppers (capsicums/bell peppers) of various colours, Asian greens like choy sum, gai laan and bok choy, several types of chilli pepper and a wealth of other delights.

Even the humble potato has gained a new reputation. After years of having to settle for 'a bag of spuds', the home cook can now choose from several different varieties, and astute retailers are able to recommend a particular type for a specific use.

Few people question the regional origins of their vegetables, but it's a different story when it comes to fruit. Cherries and apricots from Central Otago, peaches and nashi from Hawke's Bay, apples and pears from Nelson – each region has its devotees.

And we're still only scratching the surface. The New Zealand climate is ideal for growing almost anything, which means the future looks ever more exciting.

The experts tell us we should eat five-plus serves of fruit and vegetables a day. It's easy with produce like this.

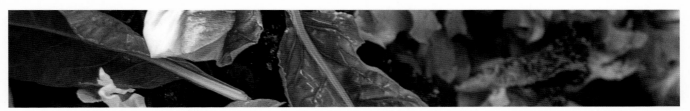

Vegetables and Salads

Good for you, and simply delicious

Organic Tofu Vegetable Stir-fry

4–6 peruperu (purple) potatoes, boiled and kept warm, or brown rice

$^1/_4$ cup light vegetable oil

$^1/_2$ medium onion, peeled and sliced

$^1/_2$ block firm tofu,* cut into 2$^1/_2$ cm cubes

1 medium carrot, peeled and cut into matchstick-sized pieces

2 medium courgettes (zucchini), thinly sliced

$^1/_2$ head broccoli, cut into florets

1 cup red cabbage, cut into 2cm squares

1 cup green cabbage, cut into 2cm squares

1 medium kumara (sweet potato), peeled, parboiled and cut into 2cm cubes

3 cloves garlic, peeled, finely crushed and chopped to a purée

2 slices peeled ginger, finely crushed and chopped to a purée

1 tablespoon miso paste*

$^1/_2$ cup diluted tamari* (60% tamari, 40% water)

1 cup vegetable stock

1 tablespoon freshly chopped herbs (mint, dill, basil, etc.)

1 tablespoon sesame seeds

Heat a wok to medium-to-high, add the oil, and cook the onion, tofu and carrot until the onion is soft but not at all browned. Add the courgettes, broccoli, red and green cabbage, kumara, garlic and ginger. Cook, stirring continuously, for 3–4 minutes. Add the miso paste, tamari and stock. Cover and cook for 3–4 minutes. Add the herbs and toss to mix.

To serve:
Divide the vegetable stir-fry, with plenty of sauce, between four heated bowls. Serve with peruperu potatoes or brown rice. Sprinkle with sesame seeds.

Serves 2

MUSICAL KNIVES, AUCKLAND

* Asian ingredients are available at Asian food stores.

Goat Cheese and Leek Fondue

with Dried Olives and Horseradish Toast

500g leeks, white part only
50g softened butter or 3 tablespoons olive oil
¹/₂ medium onion, peeled and thinly sliced
3 cloves garlic, peeled, crushed and chopped
¹/₂ teaspoon fennel seeds, crushed
100ml vegetable stock
150ml cream
50g horseradish, freshly grated
4 thin slices good quality sourdough bread, very lightly toasted
2 x 100g logs goat cheese
sea salt and freshly ground black pepper
50g freshly grated parmesan cheese
20 black olives, pitted, sliced and dried in a warm oven until leathery
¹/₄ cup chopped chives

Cut the leeks into 2cm discs. Heat a tablespoon of the butter or olive oil in a heavy-based saucepan and cook the onion, leeks, garlic and fennel seeds, turning carefully to prevent the leeks from falling apart. Add the vegetable stock and cover. Cook gently until the leeks are soft, then add half the cream. Reduce by half again, cool and reserve.

Mix the remaining butter and olive oil with the horseradish and spread on the lightly toasted bread.

Cut the goat cheese logs in half.

To serve:
Preheat the grill. Season the leek mixture to taste and carefully fold in the parmesan cheese. Divide among four shallow heatproof bowls and add one tablespoon of the remaining cream to each bowl. Place the goat cheese on top and grill until golden and heated through. Serve with the horseradish toast, sprinkled with the dried olives and chives.

Serves 4

BARCELONA BISTRO AND BAR

Garden Salad

More of a concept than a recipe, this is a tribute to fine New Zealand produce from Musical Knives' owner/ chef, Peter Chaplin. Quantities depend on the number of people you are serving.

potatoes, peeled and cut into chunks
kumara (sweet potato), peeled and cut into chunks
beetroot, scrubbed
broccoli, cut into florets, stems peeled
pumpkin, peeled and diced
cauliflower, cut into florets
beans, trimmed at the stem end only
asparagus, peeled from 1cm below the head, with the hard base end snapped off

tomatoes, cut into wedges
baby spinach leaves
fancy lettuce leaves, torn
fresh green herbs such as parsley and chervil, chopped
sea salt and freshly ground black pepper
lemon juice
extra virgin olive oil

Peter explains that the traditional technique is to plunge anything that grows above the ground (the broccoli, cauliflower, beans and asparagus) into salted water at a rolling boil, and anything that grows below the ground (the potatoes, kumara and beetroot) into cold salted water, which is then brought to the boil. Remember you are cooking the vegetables for a room-temperature salad, so they should retain a little firmness.

Arrange the cooked and raw vegetables on a platter, sprinkle with the herbs, sea salt and freshly ground pepper and drizzle with the lemon juice and olive oil. Peter's philosophy is to create 'colour, chemistry, composition and architecture – a magical plate that is a feast for your eyes as well as your mouth'.

MUSICAL KNIVES, AUCKLAND

Eggplant Stack

Basil Pesto

1 cup fresh basil leaves, chopped
1/2 cup extra virgin olive oil
1/2 cup grated parmesan cheese
2 cloves garlic, peeled, crushed and finely chopped

Combine all ingredients, using a mortar and pestle. The job can be done in a blender or food processor, but don't over-process – a bit of chunkiness is desirable.

Panadori (rich tomato sauce)

2 tablespoons olive oil
1 large onion, peeled and thinly sliced
2–3 cloves garlic, peeled, crushed and finely chopped
440g can Italian plum tomatoes
1 teaspoon dried basil
1 cup red wine
2 teaspoons sugar
sea salt and cracked black pepper

Heat the oil in a heavy-based frypan and cook the onion and garlic until soft but not coloured.

Stir in the tomatoes, roughly chopped, and their juice. Add the dried basil and red wine, cover and simmer for 50 minutes.

Add the sugar, seasoning to taste and simmer for a further 10 minutes. Keep warm.

Eggplant Discs

1 eggplant (aubergine)
sea salt and cracked pepper
2 tablespoons olive oil
400g mozzarella or bocconcini cheese

Cut the eggplant into 1cm-thick discs and season. Pan-fry in the olive oil until lightly browned on both sides. Slice the mozzarella or bocconcini 5mm thick, and place on top of each eggplant disc. Grill until cheese is melted and golden.

Mushrooms

8 flat mushrooms
2 tablespoons olive oil
sea salt and cracked black pepper

Brush mushrooms with oil and season. Pan-fry or grill whole and keep warm.

To serve:
12 black olives

Divide the panadori among four well-heated plates. Place one eggplant disc on top of each serving of sauce, and top in turn with a mushroom. Repeat the process until all ingredients are used. Garnish with olives.

Serves 4

Café Ujazi, Napier

Spinach and Feta Pikelets with Grilled Bacon and Roasted Flat Mushrooms

4 eggs
$^1/_4$ cup cream
420g can creamed corn
8 tablespoons self-raising flour
$^1/_4$ cup chopped herbs (parsley, chives, etc.)
1 tablespoon sweet chilli sauce
$1^1/_2$ loosely packed cups finely chopped spinach leaves
100g feta cheese, crumbled*
Maldon sea salt and freshly ground white pepper
olive oil
8 rashers good quality bacon
16 cherry tomatoes
8 flat mushrooms, wiped clean, stalks mostly removed*

Separate eggs and put whites aside.

Mix together the egg yolks, cream, corn, flour, herbs, chilli sauce and spinach. Stir well.

Beat the egg whites until fluffy, then fold into the mixture. Add the feta cheese, season well and refrigerate.

When the mixture is chilled, oil a very hot griddle pan and ladle tablespoonfuls of the mixture on to form pikelets. Cook for approximately 2 minutes each side, or until golden brown (taste one to make sure the timing is right).

Grill the bacon, bake the tomatoes until they are slightly wilted, and season and grill the mushrooms. Keep warm.

To serve:
Heat a large platter and layer the pikelets, bacon and mushrooms. Garnish with the tomatoes.

Serves 8 generously, or 30 as finger food if you make smaller pikelets, and top with chopped bacon and mushrooms and a halved cherry tomato

* The Old Winery Café strongly supports local providers, and uses only Kingsmeade Lark feta and Parkvale mushrooms.

THE OLD WINERY CAFÉ, MARTINBOROUGH

Merlot Roast Pear and Rocket Salad

with Balsamic Dried Tomato, Fresh Walnuts and Blue Cheese Dressing

4 tomatoes
100ml Balsamic vinegar
salt and pepper
200g fresh walnuts
2 tablespoons olive oil
4 pears (Packham or nashi)
$^1/_2$ cup merlot wine
2 tablespoons brown sugar
2 tablespoons redcurrant jelly
2 cups rocket leaves
1 red-leaf lettuce
1 green-leaf lettuce (not iceberg)

Slice tomatoes in three, drizzle with Balsamic vinegar and season. Heat the oven to 200°C, place the tomatoes on a rack with a tray underneath, turn the oven off and leave overnight, without opening the door. (Extra tomatoes can be dried at the same time but use within 1–2 days.)

Toss the walnuts in the olive oil, season lightly and roast in a 180°C oven for 5 minutes. Reserve.

Core the pears and cut into quarters. Put in an oven dish with the merlot, brown sugar and redcurrant jelly. Roast for 10–15 minutes at 180°C.

Dressing
2 egg yolks
100ml cider vinegar
300ml olive oil
100g blue cheese
salt and pepper

Put the egg yolks and cider vinegar into a food processor, and with the motor running drizzle in the olive oil. Add the cheese and season to taste.

To serve:
Wash the rocket and lettuce leaves and arrange on four plates. Place the tomatoes, walnuts and pears in and around the leaves. Drizzle dressing over the top.

Serves 4

ANNIE'S WINE BAR AND RESTAURANT, CHRISTCHURCH

Organic Roast Salad

1 parsnip, peeled
1 carrot, peeled
$^1/_2$ swede, peeled
1 beetroot, peeled
$^1/_2$ cup black olives
leaves stripped from 2 sprigs of rosemary or thyme
sea salt
$^1/_2$ cup olive oil
4 potatoes, peeled or scrubbed, depending on the type
2 kumara (sweet potatoes), peeled
$^1/_4$ medium pumpkin, unpeeled
1 whole head of garlic, separated into cloves*

You will need two roasting trays. Cut the parsnip, carrot, swede and beetroot into batons the size of thick matchsticks. Arrange on a baking tray with the olives and half the rosemary or thyme, sprinkle with sea salt and toss in half the olive oil.

Cut the potatoes, kumara and pumpkin into rough chunks, place on the second tray with the garlic cloves, remaining herbs, seasoning and oil.

Roast both trays at 180ºC for 1 hour, turning two or three times during that period.

* The garlic cloves can be peeled or not, as you prefer. If left unpeeled, guests can squeeze out the softened interior.

To serve:
fancy lettuce leaves
$^1/_2$ iceberg lettuce
lemon juice
sea salt

Thoroughly wash and dry the lettuces. Arrange the fancy leaves on four plates, finely slice the iceberg lettuce and place in the middle. Season with sea salt, then arrange a serving of roasted vegetables over the top. Finish with a squeeze of lemon juice.

MUSICAL KNIVES, AUCKLAND

Cheese

Slice it, nibble on it,
cook with it

Cheese – a truly versatile food.

Outspoken New Zealand parliamentarian, Dame Mabel Howard, once paraphrased a popular hymn when she said in the House, 'Oh, what a friend we have in cheeses.'

Irreverent it may have been, but her comment was very true. Exports of many products were down, members were being told, but the figures for cheese were way up.

Cheese has been an important earner of export dollars for our farming community almost as long as cows have been raised in this country. Our animals live outdoors, feeding on grass all year round, and that means their milk and the cheese made from it is pure and natural – a big asset in a health-conscious world.

Today, not all the cheese is made from cow's milk. An increasing number of products are made from the milk of sheep and goats, and they make a worthwhile addition to any cheeseboard.

But, of course, putting cheese on a board is only one of its uses. This most versatile of foodstuffs is good for cooking, as a snack, or even as a full meal when accompanied by a selection of pickles and chutneys, a fresh garden salad and a few interesting breads.

That's the time to feature three or four different types of cheese, and there's plenty to choose from. When the cheese is being served as part of a multi-course meal, offer it after the main course, but before dessert. That way, the last of the dry wine can be enjoyed as an accompaniment. And don't get too complicated. Often, just one cheese in perfect condition, or perhaps two of the same type, are all that is needed.

Offering cheese instead of dessert is a realistic alternative. Scatter a few sweet nibbles like fresh and dried fruit or even chocolates around the cheeseboard and your guests will be well satisfied.

And one final tip: serve crackers by all means, but also offer bread. Many people prefer it, and with the huge range of different styles available nowadays, it can be a feature in its own right.

MILD CUMIN $12.00/KG

MEDIUM CUMIN $14.00/KG

MATURE CUMIN $16.00/KG

EXTRA MATURE CUMIN $18.00/KG

Desserts

All you need for a sweet ending

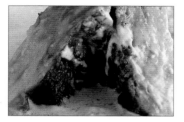

Pear and Almond Tart

Pastry

300g plain flour
pinch of salt
50g ground almonds
175g chilled butter, diced
100g icing sugar
3 egg yolks

Filling

350g softened butter
350g brown sugar
350g ground almonds
3 eggs
3 tablespoons Calvados or Frangelico liqueur
6 ripe pears, peeled, cored and halved

First, make the pastry. Pulse the flour, salt, almonds and butter in a food processor until it reaches the texture of coarse breadcrumbs. Add the sugar and egg yolks and continue to pulse until the mixture clumps together. Remove and press into a ball, wrap in plastic food wrap and chill for 30 minutes.

To make the filling, cream the butter and sugar until the mixture is pale and fluffy. Add the almonds, then beat in the eggs one at a time. Stir in the liqueur.

To assemble, press the chilled pastry into a springform tin and bake blind at 180°C for 20 minutes, or until golden. Allow to cool slightly. Cover the base with the

pears, cut side down, then pour the filling over the top. Reduce the oven temperature to 150°C and bake for 1 hour. Cool and serve with Frangelico cream (recipe below).

Frangelico Cream

250ml cream
250ml sour cream
2 tablespoons brown sugar
2 tablespoons Frangelico liqueur

Whip all ingredients together until mixture reaches soft peak stage.

Toffee Crab Apples (optional)

$^2/_3$ cup sugar
$^1/_2$ cup water
crab apples

Dissolve the sugar in the water and boil, without stirring, until the mixture is golden. Remove from the heat, and dip the cleaned and dry crab apples into it. Arrange on top of the tart.

Serves 4–6

TOAD'S LANDING, WAIRARAPA

Bread and Butter Pudding

with whisky sauce

Note: This is a bread and butter sauce without butter. Because croissants, made with butter, are used instead of bread, there is no need to add any extra. The chef who created it likes it super-creamy – you may prefer to use less cream.

4 croissants
100g sultanas, or any other dried fruit
4 eggs
1 teaspoon real vanilla essence
200g sugar
1 litre cream

Topping
100g caster sugar
1 teaspoon ground cinnamon

Whisky Sauce
¹/₂ cup sugar
¹/₄ cup water
50ml whisky
500ml cream

Slice the croissants 1cm thick and layer in a 15cm ovenproof dish. Scatter the sultanas over the top.

Mix the eggs, vanilla essence and sugar until the sugar is dissolved. Stir in the cream, then pour the mixture over the croissants and sultanas. Press lightly with a spoon to ensure the croissants are well saturated.

Mix the caster sugar and cinnamon together and sprinkle over the top. Bake at 180ºC for 45 minutes, or until the egg mixture is cooked and set.

Just before it has finished cooking, make the sauce. Put the sugar and the water into a saucepan and boil until it dissolves and turns golden. Remove from the heat and whisk in the whisky and cream.

To serve:
Divide the pudding among four heated bowls and pour the whisky sauce over the top.

Serves 4

BIG TIME CAFÉ

Baked Feijoa and Kiwifruit Tartlets

Dough
250g flour
20g cornflour
20g caster sugar
pinch of sea salt
250g unsalted butter
1 egg

In a food processor mix the dry ingredients with the butter until the mixture resembles coarse breadcrumbs. Mix the egg with a little cold water and add to the mixture. Process until the dough forms a ball and comes cleanly away from the sides, adding more water if necessary. Place on a plate and cover with plastic food wrap, then refrigerate for an hour.

When well chilled, take from the refrigerator and roll into a sheet with a rolling pin. Cut out six 9cm rounds and bake blind for approximately 20 minutes at 200°C. Don't let them get too brown.

Filling
6 feijoas, peeled and sliced
6 kiwifruit, peeled and sliced
caster sugar
whipped cream

To complete and serve:
Layer the two fruits, alternating, on the pastry rounds, sprinkle with a little caster sugar and bake for 10–12 minutes at 220°C. Top with a spoonful of whipped cream and serve.

Serves 4

MERLOT WINE CAFÉ, AUCKLAND

Bitter Chocolate
Torte with Pear and Blackcurrant Compote and Lime and Coconut Sorbet

Torte
250g top-quality dark chocolate
500ml cream

Melt the chocolate in the top half of a double boiler, lightly whip the cream and fold into the chocolate one-third at a time. When it is fully incorporated, pour into a shallow cake tin and refrigerate for 4–24 hours (the longer the better).

Compote
2 large ripe pears
200ml stock syrup (100g sugar boiled in 100ml water)
300g blackcurrants
30ml cassis liqueur, or similar

Peel and core the pears and cut into 1cm dice. Simmer in 50ml of the stock syrup until just cooked but still firm. Add blackcurrants and cook to the consistency of very light jam. Cool slightly, then stir in the cassis liqueur.

Sorbet
100ml coconut liqueur (e.g. Malibu)
100ml fresh lime juice
100ml coconut milk

Mix the coconut liqueur, lime juice, coconut milk and remaining stock syrup and put into an ice cream machine, or onto a low-sided tray. Churn to the 'soft ice' stage in the machine, or freeze on the tray, stirring frequently with a fork.

To serve:
small quantity cocoa, preferably Dutch

Cut the torte into wedges, dust with cocoa and place on plates. Warm the compote and place on the side. Form the sorbet into balls and arrange on top.

Serves 6–8

Barcelona Bistro and Bar, Christchurch

Saint Clair Butterscotch Pie

375g cream cheese, stirred to soften
$^3/_4$ cup sugar
1 teaspoon cinnamon
$^1/_4$ cup golden syrup
1 teaspoon vanilla essence
3 eggs, lightly beaten with a fork
$^1/_2$ cup sour cream
2 cups mashed cooked pumpkin
$^3/_4$ cup plain flour
400g sweet short pastry
butter for greasing
1 cup cream
2 tablespoons of your favourite liqueur

Preheat the oven to 180°C, or 160°C on fan-bake.
   Blend together the cream cheese, sugar and cinnamon.
   Add the golden syrup, vanilla essence, eggs, sour cream, mashed pumpkin and flour and blend well.

   Roll out the pastry and place in a buttered flan tin. Pour in the pumpkin mixture.
   Bake until the centre is firm – about 35 minutes.

To serve:
Whip the cream with the liqueur, divide the pie into serving pieces and top with the cream.

Serves 6–8

SAINT CLAIR, MARLBOROUGH

113

Remember when the choice was between white and wholemeal, sliced or unsliced? That's hard to imagine now. The bakery section of any supermarket will offer dozens of different styles, some pre-packaged, some made fresh daily. Crisp rolls studded with sun-dried tomatoes or olives? Of course! A pumpkin seed loaf for the breakfast toast? Why not!

Bread and baking
Food for sharing

Bread has been part of our diet since the days when we had to chase the meat that went with it. Today there is a huge variety to choose from.

We have been baking cakes and sharing them with friends and family since our pioneer days. Nowadays we are more likely to buy cakes from a shop, but there's something special about creating our own sweet snacks.

Specialist bakeries take the whole process several steps further. The baguette, once rare, has become ubiquitous. Now, we can choose any one of a dozen other French-style alternatives, or head for Italy, Spain, Portugal or the Middle East.

And breadmaking has returned as a home activity. It takes time, but there is something calming about steadily kneading a lump of dough – just the therapy we need as an antidote to today's hectic lifestyle. Best of all, the finished product is invariably delicious, and is certain to win praise from family and friends.

Of course, not all baking is time-consuming. A couple of recipes in this book call for Maori bread. Quick and tasty, it is great fun to make and even more fun to eat.

Cake making has long been part of the New Zealand homeowner's repertoire, although the increasing pace of modern life means few people bother to bake a couple of times a week, as our grandparents did. But it is worth putting time aside, say once a month, to create something special. Offering family and friends a slice or wedge of cake made with your own hands is the ultimate in hospitality.

Baking
A great New Zealand tradition

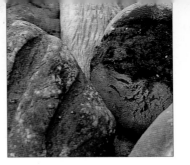

Banana Chocolate Dream

375g brown sugar
100g sour cream
100g butter
3 eggs, separated
2–3 bananas, mashed, plus 1 for garnish
160g wholemeal flour
200g plain flour
20g (2 tablespoons) baking powder
pinch of salt
a few drops lemon essence
a few drops vanilla essence
85g chocolate chips
30g white sugar
extra brown sugar
apricot jam, for glazing

Cream together the brown sugar, sour cream and butter. Add the egg yolks, then the mashed bananas. Stir in all the dry ingredients except the white sugar, along with the flavouring essences and chocolate chips.

Make a meringue by beating the egg whites and white sugar together to form stiff, shiny peaks, then fold into the mixture. Pour into a lined and greased 23cm tin with 6cm sides. Slice the reserved banana lengthways, and place on top. Cook on the middle rack of a 150°C oven and cook for 30 minutes. Sprinkle with brown sugar and cook for a further 30 minutes, or until a knife inserted into the centre comes out clean.

Heat the apricot jam and brush over the top. Cool on a cake rack

Makes 12 generous slices

SCHWARZWALD KONDITOREI, AUCKLAND

Soda Bread

350g wholemeal flour (preferably coarse)
150g plain white flour
15g bran
1¹/₂ teaspoons baking soda
pinch of salt
1 tablespoon honey
3 cups cultured buttermilk

Preheat the oven to 200°C.

Stir all the dry ingredients together. Add the honey and
pour in the buttermilk and stir to achieve a good
'dropping' consistency. Pour into a well-greased loaf tin
and bake for approximately 1 hour. Turn out onto a
wire rack and cool.

Makes one 1kg loaf

TIMARA LODGE, BLENHEIM

Blueberry and Yoghurt Slice

150g oats
150g rye flour
100g butter
2 tablespoons honey
500ml natural yoghurt
$^1/_2$ teaspoon arrowroot
100g blueberries
10g agar-agar strands (available at Asian food stores)
1 cup apple juice

Mix the oats, flour, butter, and 1 tablespoon of the honey together and press into a 25cm flan tin. Mix the remaining tablespoon of honey with the yoghurt and arrowroot, spread over the base and cook in a 180°C oven for approximately 40 minutes, or until set. Cool.

   Place the blueberries and agar-agar in a small saucepan and cover with apple juice. Simmer until well dissolved, then pour over the flan. Refrigerate until set.

Makes 1 x 25cm flan

FOOD FOR LIFE, AUCKLAND

Croissants

1 teaspoon sugar
175ml warm water
1 tablespoon yeast
500g 'strong' (unbleached) flour
2 teaspoons salt
25g lard
1 large egg, lightly beaten
150g butter

Egg Wash
1 large egg
2 tablespoons water
¹/₂ teaspoon sugar

Dissolve the sugar in the warm water and sprinkle the yeast over the top. Leave for 10 minutes, or until frothy (if it doesn't froth, start again).

Sieve together the flour and salt and rub in the lard. Add the egg and yeast liquid and mix. Knead well to form a smooth dough. Roll out to a rectangle approximately 50cm x 15cm.

Divide the butter into three portions. Dot the top two-thirds of the dough with one part of the butter, as if making flaky pastry. Fold the dough in three, as if making puff pastry, and roll. Repeat, using the other portions of butter between rollings, then repeat the whole folding and rolling process three more times.

Place in a plastic bag and refrigerate for at least an hour.

Shaping
To shape the croissants, roll the dough out to a rectangle slightly larger than 45cm x 30cm, cover with oiled plastic food wrap or a damp cloth and leave for 10 minutes. Trim the edges and divide in half lengthways. Cut each strip into three squares, then each square into two triangles.

Beat the egg with the water and sugar and brush over the triangles. Roll each triangle loosely towards the point, finishing with the tip underneath. Curve into a crescent shape. Brush with egg wash and place on ungreased baking sheets.

Cover with a damp cloth and leave in a warm place to rise (about 30 minutes). Brush again with egg wash and bake in a 220°C oven for 20 minutes, or until golden brown.

Makes 12

Food for Life, Auckland

Pavlova

4 egg whites (use older eggs, at room temperature)
pinch of salt
2 cups sugar
1 teaspoon vanilla essence
1 teaspoon vinegar
1 tablespoon cornflour
3 tablespoons boiling water

Preheat the oven to 150°C.

Beat all ingredients together in an electric mixer for 15 minutes until the mixture forms firm, glossy peaks.

Spoon the mixture onto greased baking paper on a tray in one large circle or eight small ones. Bake for 30 minutes, then turn the oven off and leave the pavlova inside for at least another hour. Do not open the oven during this time.

To serve:
Place onto plates and garnish with whipped cream and fresh fruit.

SCHWARZWALD KONDITOREI, AUCKLAND

Organics
Leading the way in the new millennium

O rganics are big. The media feeds us a steady stream of articles and broadcasts about the possible effects of this or that herbicide or pesticide on our health. Television beams pictures of cattle infected by mad cow disease, apparently caused by their feed, into our homes. It's little wonder that many people are seeking more natural alternatives.

And growers and farmers are listening. Organic butcheries are still rare, but most of our major cities boast a handful. It's a different story with fruit and vegetables. Not only have dozens of specialist outlets sprung up around the country, but many greengrocers and even supermarkets now have sections devoted to organic produce.

A small but vociferous group argues that New Zealand should become totally organic, at least as far as our exports are concerned. Financial experts say it's an impossible dream, but it has a lot of appeal. After all, we already enjoy the reputation of being clean and green, and certainly our cattle, sheep and other animals lead a far healthier lifestyle than their cousins in the US, where feedlots and giant barns are their home. Our animals eat all-natural grass. In many countries, their feed is mixed by the farmer, which means additives can be included at will.

Many of the chefs who have contributed recipes to this book use organic produce whenever they can. We should applaud them – it is definitely the way of the future.

ACKNOWLEDGEMENTS

Good Food New Zealand Style is a cookbook developed by the team who produced *New Zealand Food, Wine & Art,* together with Vic Williams who adapted the recipes for home use and wrote the features text.

This introduction to New Zealand-style food was again photographed by specialist food photographer Ian Baker.

I would particularly like to thank the chefs and managers of restaurants and cafés who supplied the recipes and presented the food for the photographic sessions. They were generous with their time and their recommendations of colleagues who could contribute to this book. A special thanks to Bridget Davis of Merlot Wine Café and Number Five for help with the cover photograph. A detailed list of participants can be found on page 4.

Once again we have a team of talented people who made this book possible. They are Ian Baker, photographer; Vic Williams, text writer and recipe editor; Barbara Nielsen, publishing manager; Lesley Coomer, designer; Silva Bassett and Diane Lowther, editorial team; and my assistant Robin Falconer.

Finally a big thank you to Joan Mackenzie of Whitcoulls for her help and encouragement.

Cliff Josephs
Publisher

Chanel Publishers Ltd
8 Binnacle Rise, Gulf Harbour
P.O. Box 403, Whangaparaoa
Auckland, New Zealand

First published by Chanel Publishers Ltd, 2001
© Photography: Ian Baker
© Text: Chanel Publishers Ltd
© Recipes: Remain with the contributing restaurants

Publisher: Cliff Josephs
Publishing manager: Barbara Nielsen
Photographer: Ian Baker
Text writer and recipe editor: Vic Williams
Design and layout: Lesley Coomer
Editorial staff: Silva Bassett and Diane Lowther
Printed by: Midas Printing (Asia) Ltd.

ISBN: 0-958208-45-X

All rights reserved. No part of this publication may be reproduced, stored in a retrieval system, or transmitted in any form or by any means, electronic, mechanical, photocopying, recording or otherwise, without the prior permission in writing of the publishers and copyright holders.

While the publishers and contributors have made every effort to ensure that the information and instruction in this book are accurate and safe, they cannot accept liability for any resulting injury or loss or damage to property whether direct or consequential.

P9-DNH-594

Good Food
New Zealand Style